Charles Dickens
OLIVER TWIST

essay by
Deborah Condon
The Dickens Project
University of California at Santa Cruz

ACCLAIM BOOKS
STUDY GUIDE

Oliver Twist

art by Arnold Hicks
adaptation by Georgina Campbell

For Classics Illustrated Study Guides
computer recoloring by VanHook Studios
editor: Madeleine Robins
assistant editor: Gregg Sanderson
design: Scott Friedlander

Classics Illustrated: Oliver Twist © Twin Circle Publishing Co.,
a division of Frawley Enterprises; licensed to First Classics, Inc.
All new material and compilation © 1997 by Acclaim Books, Inc.

Dale-Chall R.L. 8.35

ISBN 1-57840-015-5

Acclaim Books, New York, NY
Printed in the United States

STUDY GUIDE

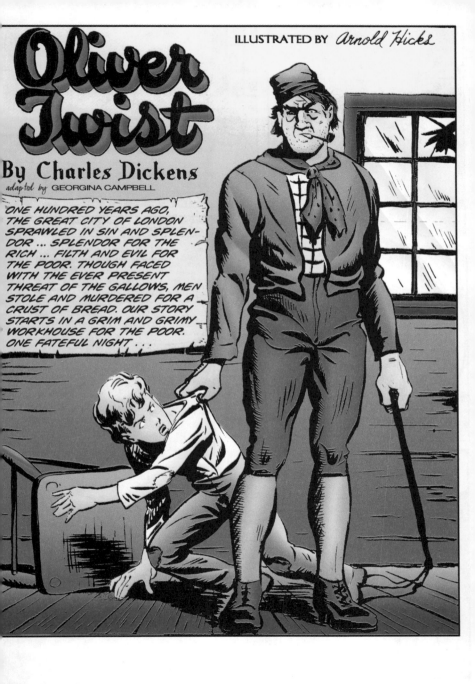

Oliver Twist

By Charles Dickens

adapted by GEORGINA CAMPBELL

ILLUSTRATED BY *Arnold Hicks*

ONE HUNDRED YEARS AGO, THE GREAT CITY OF LONDON SPRAWLED IN SIN AND SPLENDOR ... SPLENDOR FOR THE RICH ... FILTH AND EVIL FOR THE POOR. THOUGH FACED WITH THE EVER PRESENT THREAT OF THE GALLOWS, MEN STOLE AND MURDERED FOR A CRUST OF BREAD. OUR STORY STARTS IN A GRIM AND GRIMY WORKHOUSE FOR THE POOR. ONE FATEFUL NIGHT ...

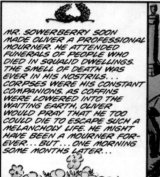

MR. SOWERBERRY SOON MADE OLIVER A PROFESSIONAL MOURNER. HE ATTENDED FUNERALS OF PEOPLE WHO DIED IN SQUALID DWELLINGS. THE SMELL OF DEATH WAS EVER IN HIS NOSTRILS... CORPSES WERE HIS CONSTANT COMPANIONS. AS COFFINS WERE LOWERED INTO THE WAITING EARTH, OLIVER WOULD PRAY THAT HE TOO COULD DIE TO ESCAPE SUCH A MELANCHOLY LIFE. HE MIGHT HAVE BEEN A MOURNER FOREVER... BUT... ONE MORNING SOME MONTHS LATER...

IN THE POLICE COURT...

WHAT IS THE CHARGE AGAINST THIS BOY?

I HAVE NO WISH TO CHARGE HIM, MR. FANG. I DID NOT SEE HIM STEAL MY HANDKERCHIEF... BESIDES... I FEAR HE IS ILL!

HE'S FAINTED!

LET HIM LIE THERE! HE'LL SOON BE TIRED OF THAT! THREE MONTHS HARD LABOR! CLEAR THE OFFICE!

WHAT!!

STOP! DON'T TAKE HIM AWAY!

WHAT IS THIS? WHO ARE YOU?

I KEEP THE BOOK-STALL... I SAW IT ALL! MR. FANG, YOU MUST HEAR ME! YOU MUST NOT REFUSE, SIR!

WHAT HAVE YOU TO SAY?

I SAW THREE BOYS... TWO OTHERS AND THE PRISONER HERE... LOITERING ON THE OPPOSITE SIDE OF THE STREET, WHEN THIS GENTLE-MAN WAS READING. THE ROBBERY WAS COMMITTED BY ANOTHER... I SAW IT! THIS BOY IS INNOCENT!

THE BOY IS DISCHARGED. CLEAR THE ROOM!

POOR BOY! I'LL TAKE HIM HOME WITH ME. CALL A COACH, SOMEBODY, PRAY!

I WILL, SIR! THE POOR BOY LOOKS AS IF HE'S IN FOR A SPELL OF FEVER.

SOME WEEKS LATER...

ANOTHER YOUNG GENTLEMAN KEPT RUNNING AWAY FROM ME, TRYING TO GET TO THE POLICE... AND HE WAS HANGED BY THE NECK... HE DIED IN TERRIBLE AGONY, HE DID! I HATE INGRATITUDE OLIVER, DEAR!

I WON'T RUN AWAY... BUT I GET SO LONELY!

IF THAT'S WHAT YOU WANT... I'LL KEEP YOU COMPANY!

OLIVER, WILL YOU JAPAN MY TROTTER-CASES?

HE MEANS, CLEAN HIS BOOTS!

?

PITY YOU AIN'T A PRIG!!

HE MEANS A THIEF, OLIVER!

I'D RATHER DIE!

FASIN HAVING PREPARED OLIVER'S MIND, BY SOLITUDE AND GLOOM, TO PREFER ANY SOCIETY TO HIS OWN THOUGHTS, THE YOUTH WAS DAILY LED NEARER TO A LIFE OF CRIME. ONE DAMP, WINDY NIGHT, OLD FASIN WRAPPED HIMSELF INTO HIS GREAT-COAT AND SLID INTO THE MUDDY STREETS....

WHAT A NIGHT FOR CRIME! I HOPE BILL SIKES IS AT HOME... I HAVE A LITTLE JOB FOR HIM!

UP YOU GO TOBY.

THE BOY NEXT! HOIST HIM UP; I'LL CATCH HOLD OF HIM!

PLEASE LET ME RUN AWAY. HAVE MERCY ON ME AND DON'T MAKE ME STEAL!

GET UP, OR I'LL STREW YOUR BRAINS OUT!

SHH! NOT HERE! COME WITH ME, OLIVER!

NOW, OLIVER, I'M GOING TO PUT YOU THROUGH THIS WINDOW! TAKE THE LANTERN... GO SOFTLY UP THE STEPS, UNFASTEN THE DOOR... AND LET US IN!

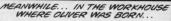

REALLY... MR. BUMBLE! I'LL SCREAM!! YOU DO HAVE A WAY WITH THE LADIES.

PLEASE COME, MISTRESS... OLD SALLY IS A-GOIN FAST. SHE SEZ SHE 'AS SOMETHIN' TO TELL WHICH YOU GOTTA 'EAR!

WHAT IS IT, SALLY?

COME NEARER, MA'AM.... IN THIS BED I ONCE NURSED A PRETTY YOUNG CREETUR'. SHE GAVE BIRTH TO A BOY, OND DIED. I STOLE A GOLD LOCKET FROM 'ER NECK! 'ER BOY WAS CALLED OLIVER... BEFORE SHE DIED SHE SAID TO ME....

SHE'S DEAD! I WONDER WHERE SHE KEPT THAT GOLD LOCKET? I'LL FIND IT, BUT NOW.... BACK TO MR. BUMBLE!

DEAR LADY, THE MASTER OF THIS WORKHOUSE IS AILING FAST! HIS DEATH WILL CAUSE A VACANCY... WHAT AN OPPORTUNITY FOR JOINING OUR HEARTS AND HOUSEKEEPING! SAY THE ONE LITTLE WORD!

Y...YE...YES!

AH! I'VE MADE A CAREFUL COUNT OF HER POSESSIONS! SHE'S A LUCKY WOMAN TO BE GETTING SO THOUGHTFUL A HUSBAND!

LATER THAT MORNING...

HAVE YOU SEEN THIS THIEF YET? HE HASN'T SHAVED, BUT HE DOESN'T LOOK AT ALL FEROCIOUS NOTWITH-STANDING!

THIS POOR CHILD THE PUPIL OF ROBBERS! WHAT CAN I DO TO SAVE HIM?

LET ME THINK.. I'LL SEE THE CONSTABLE ...BUT WE'LL GET THIS YOUNG MAN'S STORY FIRST.

YOUNG MAN, ALL I WANT IS THE TRUTH.

I WAS BORN IN A WORK-HOUSE.

I'LL SEE OLD GILES... CONFUSE HIM SO HE WON'T KNOW WHAT HE'S TALKING ABOUT!

POOR CHILD. HE'LL BE SAFE HERE!

....AND SO BILL SIKES BOUND UP MY ARM AND LEFT ME IN THE DITCH.

MR. GILES ...ARE YOU A RELIGIOUS MAN?

YES, SIR, I HOPE SO.... AND BRITTLES LIKEWISE.

THEN, CAN YOU SWEAR THAT THE BOY UPSTAIRS IS THE BOY PUT THROUGH THE WINDOW LAST NIGHT? ON YOUR SOLEMN OATH, ARE YOU ABLE TO IDENTIFY THAT BOY?

THEY DO NOT KNOW ....HAH!

IN THE COTTAGE, OLIVER SPENT THREE HAPPY MONTHS. THEN ONE MORNING...

HULLO! COME IN!

I'M HARRY MAYLIE! HELLO!

MOTHER!

HARRY! MY DEAR SON!

DOES HE STILL WANT TO MARRY ROSE?

I MUST SEE ROSE... I'VE WAITED TOO LONG... YOU KNOW I LOVE HER.

I KNOW... BUT..

ROSE IS AN ORPHAN, THOUGH I'VE ADOPTED HER. IF SHE MARRIES HARRY, IT WILL RUIN HIS POLITICAL CAREER!

THEN ONE EVENING...

MY SPIES TELL ME A YOUNG BOY HAS BEEN SEEN HERE WHO SOUNDS LIKE OLIVER.

I HOPE SO! SEE! THAT IS HE!

MR. MAYLIE! HARRY! COME QUICKLY!

...THEY RAN THAT WAY!

NO SIGN OF THEM. IT MUST HAVE BEEN A DREAM! ARE YOU SURE YOU SAW FAGIN AND THE STRANGE MAN?

YES... I'M SURE! BUT THEY'VE GONE...

NEXT MORNING...

... AND SO, DEAR ROSE, I OFFER YOU THE HEART SO LONG YOUR OWN.

NO! I CAN'T MARRY YOU!

I'M AN ORPHAN... ADOPTED BY YOUR MOTHER. YOU HAVE A GREAT PUBLIC CAREER AHEAD OF YOU. IF WE MARRIED, IT WOULD BE RUINED!

I'LL NEVER GIVE UP HOPE! NOW, THO, I MUST RETURN TO LONDON... GOODBYE... I'LL SEE YOU SOON AGAIN.

AS HARRY RETURNED TO LONDON, MR. BUMBLE WAS ACCOSTED IN A SMALL INN BY MONKS...

AND TO THINK I WAS ONCE MY OWN MASTER! MRS. BUMBLE'S A VIXEN, AND NO MISTAKE!

SHE DIED... BUT FIRST SHE GAVE MY WIFE SOME BELONGINGS.

TWELVE YEARS AGO, A BOY WAS BORN IN A WORKHOUSE, AND CHRISTENED BY YOU. WHERE IS THE OLD WOMAN WHO NURSED HIS MOTHER?

I WANT THEM AND I'LL PAY FOR THEM! YOU AND YOUR WIFE COME TO THIS ADDRESS TOMORROW EVENING AT NINE!

THAT EVENING...

THAT SHOULD BE IT!

HALLO-

FIRST GIVE ME THE GOLD!

NOW SPEAK!

BEFORE OLD SALLY DIED, SHE TOLD ME SHE HAD STOLEN A GOLD LOCKET AND WEDDING RING FROM THE BEAUTIFUL YOUNG WOMAN.

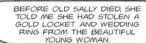

HERE THEY ARE!

AGNES

THERE! NOW GO... BOTH OF YOU!

ALL EVIDENCE OF OLIVER'S BIRTH IS NOW DESTROYED! NO ONE KNOWS HE IS MY HALF-BROTHER. I CAN LIVE ON HIS INHERITANCE WITHOUT FEAR!

COME IN!

BY LISTENING TO OTHER TALKS BETWEEN MONKS AND FAGIN, NANCY SOON KNEW OLIVER'S STORY. ONE NIGHT, SHE LEFT BILL SIKES AND CAME TO A HOTEL IN LONDON, WHERE SHE HAD OVERHEARD MONKS SAY ROSE MAYLIE AND HER AUNT WERE STAYING...

I'M THE GIRL WHO DRAGGED LITTLE OLIVER BACK TO OLD FAGIN'S ON THE NIGHT HE WENT OUT FROM MR. BROWNLOW'S HOUSE...!

YOU... HOW COULD YOU?

YET, I'VE BEEN OLIVER'S FRIEND FROM THE FIRST... AT THE RISK OF MY LIFE, I OVERHEARD A STRANGE MAN CALLED MONKS SAY OLIVER WAS HIS BROTHER... THAT THE PROOF LAY AT THE BOTTOM OF THE RIVER... THAT *YOU* WOULD GIVE THOUSANDS OF POUNDS TO KNOW WHO OLIVER REALLY IS!

STAY HERE WITH ME... DON'T GO BACK TO THOSE DREADFUL PEOPLE.

I MUST GO BACK TO BILL... HE'S ALL I HAVE TO LOVE. SHOULD YOU WANT TO QUESTION ME FURTHER, MEET ME ON LONDON BRIDGE. I'LL WALK THERE EVERY SUNDAY NIGHT, FROM ELEVEN 'TIL THE CLOCK STRIKES TWELVE... AS LONG AS I'M ALIVE!

TO WHOM CAN I TELL THIS STRANGE STORY?

I'VE SEEN MR. BROWNLOW! HE'S BACK IN LONDON! HERE'S HIS ADDRESS!

NEXT MORNING...

VERY CUNNING! I *THOUGHT* YOU WUZ YER FRIEND LAST NIGHT!

EVERY MAN'S HIS OWN FRIEND, MY DEAR! I NEED YOU, FOR MY BEST MAN WAS TOOK BY THE POLICE...POOR OLD DODGER!

HE'S BEING TRIED TODAY. TO THINK OF THE ARTFUL DODGER BEING CONDEMNED FOR A MERE SILVER SNUFF-BOX!

...AND I TELL YOU I DON'T WANT TO GO INTO COURT AND SEE WHAT HAPPENS TO THE DODGER...IT'S DANGEROUS!

NO DANGER AT ALL, MY DEAR!

HA! HA! HE LOOKS EVEN MORE OF A COUNTRY BUMPKIN THAN EVER BEFORE! GOOD LUCK, MR. BOLTER!

THE DODGER'S BEING BROUGHT IN NOW...

WOT AM I PLACED IN THIS 'ERE DISGRACEFUL SITIVATION FOR? I'VE AN APPOINTMENT WITH A GENELMAN IN THE CITY!

SILENCE!

HA! HA!

...I SAW THE PRISONER STEAL A SILVER SNUFF-BOX FROM A GENTLE-MAN'S POCKET!

HAS THE PRISONER ANYTHING TO SAY?

NO! MY ATTORNEY IS A-BREAKFASTING WITH THE WICE PRESIDENT OF THE HOUSE OF COMMONS AND...

GUILTY!

TAKE ME TO PRISON! SEE IF I CARE!

FAGIN WILL BE PLEASED TO HEAR HOW WELL DODGER BEHAVED!

MEANWHILE, NANCY GREW DAILY THINNER AND PALER. HATING FAGIN, SHE LOVED BILL SIKES. SHE KNEW IF EITHER DISCOVERED SHE WAS IN CONTACT WITH ROSE MAYLIE, SHE WOULD BE KILLED. ALTHOUGH ROSE HAD PROMISED NO HARM WOULD BEFALL ANY OF FAGIN'S GANG, NANCY WAS AFRAID....

IF I LEAVE NOW, I'LL HAVE TIME TO GO TO LONDON BRIDGE AND MEET ROSE MAYLIE...AS I PROMISED!

HALLO! WHERE'S THE GAL GOING AT THIS TIME OF NIGHT?

NOT FAR!

WHY, NANCE DEAR... YOU LOOK ILL! WHAT AILS YOU?

NOTHING... I FEEL FINE! WHAT DAY IS IT?

SUNDAY, WHY WOTS UP?

I JUST WONDERED.

NO YOU DON'T! SIT DOWN!

I'M NOT WELL... I WANT A BREATH OF AIR. LET ME GO, BILL!

DAYS PASSED. THEN ON SUNDAY EVENING...

THAT'S THE WOMAN... FOLLOW HER!

RIGHTO!

IF I HURRY, I CAN GET TO LONDON BRIDGE IN TIME!

LONDON BRIDGE...

THEY HAVEN'T COME. I'LL WAIT 'TIL TWELVE.

WHAT A NIGHT TO MEET A LOVER... THE GIRL'S MORE TROUBLE THAN SHE'S WORTH!

I'M AFRAID TO SPEAK HERE! COME DOWN YONDER STEPS!

IF THEY DON'T COME DOWN SO FAR, I CAN HEAR WITHOUT BEING SEEN!

IT FOLLOWS ME YET!

GO AWAY! GO AWAY!

I'LL RETURN TO LONDON, GET MONEY FROM FAGIN, ESCAPE TO FRANCE!

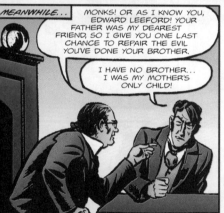

MEANWHILE...

MONKS! OR AS I KNOW YOU, EDWARD LEEFORD! YOUR FATHER WAS MY DEAREST FRIEND, SO I GIVE YOU ONE LAST CHANCE TO REPAIR THE EVIL YOU'VE DONE YOUR BROTHER.

I HAVE NO BROTHER... I WAS MY MOTHER'S ONLY CHILD!

WHEN YOUR PARENTS SEPARATED, YOUR FATHER MET A BEAUTIFUL GIRL...THEY FELL IN LOVE. HE WAS TO HAVE MARRIED HER... BUT HE DIED FIRST. BEFORE HE DIED, HE LEFT ME WITH A PORTRAIT OF THE GIRL...OLIVER'S MOTHER, AGNES FLEMING! IT TOOK ME YEARS TO FIND OLIVER, AND SEE HOW WELL YOU HAD TREATED HIM!

YOU HAVE NO PROOF!

I HAVE! EVERY WORD THAT PASSED BETWEEN FAGIN AND YOU IS KNOWN! YOU MUST DISCLOSE THE WHOLE TRUTH, SWEAR TO IT, AND RESTORE TO OLIVER HIS RIGHTFUL INHERITANCE!

I'LL DO IT...YOU LEAVE ME NO ALTER-NATIVE!

THE MURDERER OF THAT POOR GIRL WILL BE TAKEN TONIGHT! POLICE HAVE TRACKED HIM TO A LONELY HOUSE ON JACOB'S ISLAND! LET US HURRY THERE!

NANCY'S DEATH WILL BE AVENGED! I'LL ADD A REWARD OF FIFTY POUNDS TO THE HUNDRED OFFERED BY THE GOVERNMENT FOR THE MURDERER'S CAPTURE!

OLIVER IS MY HALF-BROTHER. BEFORE HE DIED, OUR FATHER GAVE ME A WILL, LEAVING HIS PROPERTY BETWEEN AGNES, OLIVER'S MOTHER, AND THEIR CHILD....OLIVER....BUT ONLY IF HE NEVER DID ANYTHING DISHONORABLE!

THAT WAS WHY YOU BRIBED FAGIN TO TRY AND MAKE A THIEF OUT OF OLIVER?

YES...I HATED THE THOUGHT OF HIM... I HAD TO HUNT HIM DOWN.

THE FATHER OF AGNES FLEMING HAD TWO CHILDREN. WHAT BECAME OF THE OTHER?

THERE SHE IS... THE GIRL YOU CALL ROSE!

THEN...I'M YOUR AUNT, OLIVER!

BUT YOU ARE MORE LIKE MY SISTER, ROSE DEAR!

THIS TIME...I WON'T TAKE NO FOR AN ANSWER!

I HAVE SOMETHING TO ASK YOU, ROSE... ALONE!

THE END.

OLIVER TWIST
CHARLES DICKENS

Charles Dickens was an ambitious young man of twenty-five when the first monthly installment of *Oliver Twist* appeared in a new magazine, *Bentley's Miscellany*, of which he was the editor. He had just quit his job as a reporter a few months before Victoria took the throne as Queen of England. It was the beginning of an era, and of a great career for Dickens, who became the most popular and celebrated author of his time.

Charles Dickens was born into a lower-middle-class family newly risen from the working class; his grandparents had been domestic servants. His father John Dickens, a clerk in the Navy Pay Office, saw himself as a man on his way up—but times were hard and the Dickens family had trouble making ends meet. John Dickens was arrested for debt and most of the family went to live with him in prison, as was the custom. Twelve-year-old Charles was left behind to work at a blacking warehouse, where his job was to paste labels on jars of boot blacking from eight in the morning until eight at night. Such arrangements were not at all uncommon; children of the working classes were expected to help support their families, and they were not exempt from the long hours that adults worked.

But for the sensitive and intelligent young Charles, who already had some education, this was a serious blow to his sense of himself and to his ambitions. He was on his own, living in a lodging house and earning so little money that he never had quite enough to eat. He spent a lot of time wandering the streets of London, observing the life there, which both fascinated and frightened him, a habit that became a life-long pastime. He later said that he felt he had narrowly escaped a fate like that of the boys in Fagin's gang.

Charles worked in the blacking warehouse for only about six months, but it must have seemed an eternity to a twelve-year-old boy who felt abandoned by his family and in despair over his future. The experience was so traumatic for Dickens that he couldn't bear to talk about it for the rest of his life. He wrote about it, however, in an autobiographical fragment, which was published after his death. We can also see the ways in which he fictionalized this experience in *Oliver Twist* and other novels: for example, in the nightmarish quality of Oliver's lonely abandonment, in Oliver's exploitation and abuse at the hands of cold and uncaring adults, and in the precariousness of Oliver's prospects in life. John Dickens was released from prison when he inherited money that enabled him to pay off his debts. Charles was then able to return to school, though he never had the opportunity to attend a university. He began working as a clerk in a law

Oliver Twist on Stage and Screen

Dramatic adaptations of *Oliver Twist* have been controversial from the first. Early stage productions, which began appearing even while the magazine serial was still originally running in 1837, were soon banned because of the violent audience reaction, especially to the murder scene. In one production, the actor playing Sikes dragged the actress playing Nancy by her hair not once, but twice, across the stage.

There have been many film versions dating back to the days of silent film, the best known being the popular academy-award-winning musical, *Oliver!*. The most controversial film adaptation is the 1948 version starring Alec Guiness as Fagin, which was protested in Europe, and was actually banned in the United States, where it was not shown until 1970 because of objections to the anti-Semitic and vaguely homosexual portrayal of Fagin.

office at the age of fifteen, then taught himself shorthand so that he could become a reporter. From there, he went on to write short sketches and fiction for magazines. His serialized novels were an immediate success, and he continued to write them to the end of his life.

Dickens was a brilliant and energetic man with many interests: he was an amateur actor and magician, social activist and traveler, as well as novelist, journalist, editor, and publisher. Dickens was fascinated with crime and criminal detection. He was even something of a police "groupie," accompanying the famous Inspector Field on cases in order to observe the life and work of a detective, which he described in a series of magazine articles.

Another passionate interest was the theater; Dickens wanted to be an actor and he had considerable talent. He acted in amateur theatricals, and later in his career he toured and gave dramatic readings from his books. One of the most popular and famous was the one that he called "Sikes and Nancy," which included a dramatization of Nancy's murder scene from *Oliver Twist*. His performance of the scene astounded audiences—women literally

fainted and had to be carried out—and exhausted Dickens to the point where his friends and family were convinced that these performances hastened his death in 1870, over thirty years after he had first created the famous scene.

Background

Oliver Twist was a new kind of novel: a realistic look at inner-city life and crime in London of the 1830s, especially the problem of juvenile gangs. The novel exposes a range of social problems: poverty, homelessness, unemployment, domestic violence, child abuse, alcoholism. These issues were controversial topics in Dickens's time, and they sound familiar to us now. Many of the problems facing England at the beginning of the 19th-century are similar to problems we face now at the end of the 20th-century.

In the 1830s the crime novel was already popular. Books with criminals as their main characters had been dubbed "Newgate novels" after the notorious Newgate prison in London and the *Newgate Calendar*, a publication telling of the lives and careers of infamous criminals. *Oliver Twist* has much in common with other Newgate novels in its criminal theme, but it also differs from them in its more realistic look at the criminal underworld. Whereas other Newgate novels tended to romanticize the criminal, Dickens's intent in *Oliver Twist* was to show criminals "as they really are." Dickens was much criticized for this; many people did not want to face the serious and growing injustices and social problems that accompanied rapid social change under industrial capitalism.

Dickens was also accused of exaggerating these conditions. And he does indeed use exaggeration, which is a common technique of satire. But he doesn't exaggerate by much: the starvation diet in a workhouse, for example, was not quite as meager as he depicts it, but was in reality woefully inadequate, consisting mostly of bread and gruel, with only a few ounces of meat and cheese per week for an adult male, and less for women and children—and almost no fruits or vegetables.

In some respects Dickens actually understates problems such as the filthy conditions in which slum dwellers lived. The human and animal excrement which littered the streets of London's slums Dickens merely hints at, referring to the "filth" and "foul odors." Dickens also considered the sexual exploitation of women and children unsuitable for graphic representation. The word "prostitute" is never used in the book to describe Nancy, but that is what she is, as Dickens frankly states in his preface. He relies instead on what he calls the "unavoidable inference" to communicate such information to his audience. This means that there is a limit to his realism; he admitted that he had to clean up the language of his criminal characters so as not to offend his audience.

It may seem prudish to us now, but Dickens practiced a form of self-censor-ship out of respect for his audience, which consisted largely of families who often read his serialized novels aloud together. He felt it was his responsibility both to entertain and educate by representing life as he observed it around him, but to do so with tact and taste. Dickens's audience devoured the monthly installments of his stories in much the same way that we avidly follow our favorite television shows today. As a result, Dickens had an enormous impact on public opinion in his society.

Characters

Oliver Twist: an orphan whose mother dies giving birth to him in a workhouse for paupers. Poor Oliver is abused, neglected, and exploited, adopted by a gang of criminals, and finally by benevolent strangers who turn out to be his long lost family and friends. Oliver isn't a strictly realistic character. According to Dickens himself, Oliver represents "the principle of good surviving through every adverse circumstance, and triumphing at last." Oliver is a figure of innocent childhood, the center of the plot, the person connecting the various social classes and communities represented in the novel.

YOUNG MAN, ALL I WANT IS THE TRUTH.

I WAS BORN IN A WORK-HOUSE.

Mr. Bumble: beadle of the local parish where Oliver is born—the kind of pompous, self-serving bureaucrat that Dickens especially despised. Mr. Bumble, as his name suggests, provides not only comic relief, but an opportunity for scathing social criticism. Cruel, cold-hearted and mercenary, he grows fat while the poor under his care starve.

Mrs. Corney: the matron in charge of the workhouse who marries Mr. Bumble and makes his life miserable. She's referred to in the Classics Illustrated adaptation as a "wealthy widow." Mrs. Corney beats Bumble up and degrades him in front of the workhouse paupers, and eventually they end up as paupers in the workhouse they once controlled.

Mrs. Mann: the woman in charge of the "branch workhouse" or "baby farm," where Oliver lives until he's nine-years-old. Women like Mrs. Mann took in infants for a fee, and while some baby farms were legitimate foster homes, many were nothing more than profit-making businesses in which many children died of neglect. Mrs. Mann's establishment is clearly one of those.

Mr. and Mrs. Sowerberry: owners of the funeral business to which Oliver is apprenticed. Mr. Sowerberry appreciates Oliver's usefulness, but Mrs. Sowerberry treats him like a slave, feeding him dog scraps and making him sleep under the counter in the coffin shop. Like Mr. Bumble, Mr. Sowerberry is bullied by a domineering wife.

Noah Claypole and Charlotte: Noah is an apprentice and Charlotte a servant in the Sowerberrys' establishment. Noah is a "charity boy," poor but not an orphan. Because he knows who his parents are, he believes he's superior to Oliver, and therefore takes every opportunity to taunt and abuse him. Noah is a thoroughly nasty character, and shows up again in London, where he joins Fagin's gang and spies for him. Charlotte attaches herself to Noah and follows him to London.

The Artful Dodger: real name, Jack Dawkins; a member of Fagin's gang of pickpockets who meets Oliver near the outskirts of London and introduces him into the gang. The Dodger is about the same age as Oliver, but much more street smart. The Dodger isn't a bad fellow, more a clown than a villain; after all, he befriends Oliver, feeds him when he's half-starved, gives him a place to stay, and never takes part in the worst of the plot against him.

Charley Bates: another young member of Fagin's gang and the Dodger's sidekick. Charley is traumatized by Nancy's murder and, perhaps as a result, goes straight in the end.

Anti-Semitism in 19th-Century England

Anti-Semitism was an ugly fact of life in 19th century England. Jews were a small minority, and at the time this book was written, did not possess the full rights and privileges of English citizenship. Most professions were closed to Jews, so they earned their livings as peddlers, merchants of used-goods, and moneylenders. Dickens defended himself against charges of anti-Semitism by pointing out that most fences of stolen goods in London were in fact Jews. But as one of his Jewish readers, a Mrs. Eliza Davis, pointed out to him, it wasn't fair to allow one very negative character to represent all Jews in his fictional world.

Dickens must have seen the truth in this criticism, for in later editions of Oliver Twist he replaced many references to "the Jew" with "Fagin"; in a much later book, *Our Mutual Friend* (1862-65), he created a more positive Jewish character, the kindly old Mr. Riah. Dickens did not want to be labeled an anti-Semite, but his attitude toward Jews was ambivalent. While he deplored persecution and oppression of Jewish people, he was known to make anti-Jewish remarks in his letters. Such remarks diminished as he grew older, perhaps as the result of his acquaintance with Jews like Mrs. Davis and her husband.

Fagin: a "fence" or trader in stolen goods, and leader of a gang of young thieves. Fagin's philosophy is to look out for "number one," and he doesn't mind sacrificing members of his gang to the gallows in order to save himself. Fagin is being paid by Monks to corrupt Oliver and make him a thief.

Fagin is a Jew, and therefore an outsider in English society of the time. There is no getting around the fact that Dickens was exploiting a long and ugly history of anti-Jewish prejudice dating back to the Middle Ages. Many superstitions and stereotypes about Jews are embodied by Fagin: Christ-killers, devils, kidnappers and murderers of Christian children; poisoners, swindlers, misers, etc. By making Fagin a Jew, Dickens used these associations to paint him as a bogeyman—and a social outcast.

Bill Sikes: a hardened criminal and professional burglar who uses Fagin as his fence. When we first see Sikes he is kicking his dog; this can be read as a sign of how he treats Nancy (and will treat Oliver). Sikes seems to be a thoroughly bad character, but he does show pangs of conscience when it's too late: after he has murdered Nancy he's haunted by guilt. He becomes almost sympathetic as we witness his gruesome fate.

Nancy: teenage prostitute and thief, member of Fagin's gang, and Bill Sikes's woman. She takes a liking to Oliver and defends him, first from Sikes's violent abuse, and ultimately from the plot to corrupt him. Nancy is a powerful figure, one of Dickens's more interesting and complex female characters. She faces the most difficult moral choice in the novel, and pays the ultimate price for doing the right thing.

Mr. Brownlow: a kind and wealthy gentleman who befriends Oliver after he has been wrongly accused of robbing Mr.

IF THAT'S WHAT YOU WANT.. I'LL KEEP YOU COMPANY!

Brownlow. In one of the astounding coincidences that drive the plot of the book, he also turns out to be the closest friend of Oliver's father, and actually has a portrait of Oliver's late mother hanging on his wall. Mr. Brownlow helps to prove Oliver's identity and eventually adopts him as his own son.

The Maylies: the family whose home Bill Sikes attempts to burglarize, with Oliver as his unwilling accomplice. In another outrageous coincidence, **Rose Maylie** turns out to be Oliver's aunt. **Mrs. Maylie** is her adoptive mother, and Mrs. Maylie's son **Harry**, an aspiring politician, is in love with Rose and wants to marry her, despite her lack of fortune or social position. Rose is supposed to be a the heroine of the novel—but she's a bit too good to be true and, as a result, is one of the less believable characters.

Monks: the mysterious stranger who seems to have it in for Oliver, and plots with Fagin to corrupt him. Monks turns out to be Oliver's half brother, Edward Leeford, who doesn't want Oliver to inherit the money left him by their father.

Plot and Themes

Oliver Twist is first and foremost a novel of social criticism. Victorian England was a nation of stark contrasts between the rich and the poor, and conditions were particularly bad at the time Dickens was writing this book. Poverty and hunger, unemployment, homelessness, disease, and crime were major problems. Even people who had jobs suffered: working conditions were unpleasant and unsafe, pay was low, hours long, and child labor was the norm, not the exception. Dickens wanted to expose the misery and despair of poor people, the injustices and cruelties they faced, and he wanted the more privileged classes to face up to the problems and do something about them.

Oliver Twist is also a book that is, in a sense, arguing with itself over the difficult philosophical question of human nature: are people inherently good (or bad), or are they products of their circumstances? The novel doesn't give any clear-cut answers. Sometimes the book seems to be suggesting that people are the products of their environment; that poverty and misery are what drive people to crime, rather than any innate moral failing. At other times, the book seems to support a more traditional view that people only make moral choices according to their natures.

The first half of the novel traces the trials of young Oliver as he's shuffled back and forth between the "respectable" and criminal worlds. The book has often been read as a moral fable, in which good and evil battle it out with Oliver as the battleground. But if we look a little closer, it's not that simple. Good and evil may at first appear to be clear-cut: Oliver is a good boy, Noah Claypole is a very bad one; Mr. Brownlow and the Maylies are kindly, respectable people, Fagin and Sikes are low-life villains, and so forth. But there are characters who don't fit so neatly into these categories. The guardians of Oliver's early childhood, Mr. Bumble, Mrs. Mann, and the Sowerberrys, are "respectable" citizens with the responsibility of caring for the welfare of the poor—who inflict misery and even death on their charges.

These early chapters satirize the harsh treatment of the poor under the New Poor Law—especially children and old people, such as the old woman who dies of starvation in the workhouse. Mrs. Corney, the workhouse mistress, is annoyed by the woman's death because it interrupts her dinner!

In *Oliver Twist* Dickens is specifically targeting the Poor Law Amendment Act of 1834, which was, essentially, welfare reform, and reduced the amount of aid to able-bodied paupers to discourage them from relying on public assistance. This is why the food rations were so meager in the workhouse: hunger and discomfort were supposed to drive paupers out to find work.

The workhouse was more like a prison than a homeless shelter: husbands and wives were separated, had to wear uniforms, and were subject to strict discipline. Workhouse inmates were forced to do menial work in exchange for meager food and shelter. The workhouse was a last resort for the down-and-out, the ultimate humiliation and failure.

At the age of nine Oliver is considered old enough to start earning his keep, and he's apprenticed to a trade. It is in the workhouse that the famous scene occurs in which Oliver dares to ask for more food. The workhouse authorities are outraged by the request, and one board member declares in disgust that Oliver is destined to be hung as a common criminal. This scene ironically foreshadows Oliver's future association with criminals, but it also satirizes the unfair criminalization of the poor. The pathos of a hungry child's modest request for more gruel is a comment on the larger issue of the rights of the poor and the working classes to a fairer share of the nation's wealth.

Oliver is treated like a criminal by the workhouse board; he's put in solitary confinement and publicly flogged as an example to the other boys. During this time he narrowly escapes being apprenticed to a chimney sweep—a "nasty trade" as one of the workhouse officials admits, one in which small boys are often suffocated to death in chimneys. Oliver is saved from this terrible fate by a kindly old magistrate, who sees Oliver's fear and refuses to approve the apprenticeship.

Oliver is finally apprenticed to the funeral business of Mr. and Mrs. Sowerberry, where he is abused by Mrs. Sowerberry, Noah Claypole, and Charlotte. When Oliver can no longer tolerate the abuse, he becomes a homeless runaway, making his way to London, where he meets Jack Dawkins—the Artful Dodger. The Dodger is different from anyone Oliver has ever known, and speaks a cockney street slang that Oliver can barely understand. He treats the half-starved Oliver to a "long and hearty meal," and offers him a free place to stay. Whatever his misgivings, Oliver can't afford to say no.

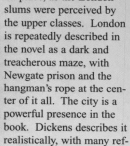

The Dodger leads Oliver to Fagin's hideout through the mean streets of London: "A dirtier or more wretched place he had never seen," where "drunken men and women were positively wallowing in filth." This is the notorious section of London called Saffron Hill, a part of town that Dickens's middle-class readers would not have dared to visit—even the police were reluctant to go there: a dangerous, forbidden place, as the London slums were perceived by the upper classes. London is repeatedly described in the novel as a dark and treacherous maze, with Newgate prison and the hangman's rope at the center of it all. The city is a powerful presence in the book. Dickens describes it realistically, with many references to actual places, yet also endows it with a nightmare quality that gives the book a psychological dimension as well.

So Oliver is adopted by a gang of criminals who subject him to a new kind of apprenticeship: he's trained to become a pickpocket and burglar. Oliver is so innocent that he thinks his training as a thief is just a "queer game."

One of the great ironies of the novel is the question of which group of "guardians" is worse: the cruel and corrupt officials to whom the government entrusts Oliver, or the criminals who find

Nancy as Battered Woman

Domestic abuse isn't a new phenomenon, and we recognize in Nancy the "battered woman's syndrome": devotion to, and dependence on, the man who beats her, as well as a fatalistic fear that she can never escape him, even if she wants to. Dickens would not have known the term "battered woman's syndrome," but he knew the phenomenon. The real-

life inspiration for Nancy may have been a young woman Dickens saw in a hospital, whom he described in his book *Sketches by Boz*. Dying of injuries inflicted by her lover, this woman refused to press charges, not wanting him to go to prison. It may have been this woman Dickens had in mind when he insisted that the portrait of Nancy "*is true.*"

him wandering the streets. Both groups abuse and exploit him, both groups endanger his life. The reader is tempted to prefer the criminals: Fagin's den may be a sinister place, but there's plenty of food and laughter, both of which were in short supply at the workhouse.

But then another group of guardians comes into the picture: the respectable members of the upper classes. Wealthy and benevolent, they befriend Oliver and help him to find his rightful place in the world. They seem to be there whenever Oliver is in danger of giving in to the criminal life, and they are introduced through a series of extraordinary coincidences.

Mr. Brownlow rescues Oliver from the gang the first time, when Oliver is mistakenly arrested for robbing him. Mr. Brownlow, however, is encouraged by his cynical and suspicious friend Grimwig to test Oliver's innocence by allowing the boy to go back out on the streets unchaperoned. The test reveals these men's ignorance of real life on the streets: they see Oliver's dilemma as one of moral choice, but for him it's a matter of survival. He promptly falls back into the clutches of Sikes and Nancy, who are there waiting for him.

In the scene that follows (Chapter 16 in the novel) we see a different side to Nancy's character: her sensitivity, vulnerability, and her devotion to Sikes. As they pass Newgate prison, Nancy declares that if Sikes were inside waiting to be hung, she would faithfully stand vigil outside. (The prison isn't mentioned by name—Dickens's contemporary readers would have known exactly what was meant.)

Nancy is another important character who doesn't fit neatly into any moral category. She's a "fallen" woman who would have been considered absolutely outcast from respectable society; yet Nancy turns out to be one of the most generous and courageous figures in the book. To modern readers Nancy seems a truer heroine than Rose Maylie, for she takes a more active role in protecting Oliver, and she makes the greater sacrifice, one requiring real courage. But perhaps both "heroines" together embody the spirit of Oliver's mother, an idealized figure whose portrait in Mr. Brownlow's house looks down upon Oliver like a guardian angel.

The strict moral code of the Victorians, with its sexual double standard, condemned women like Nancy and Oliver's mother, Agnes, on moral grounds—yet Dickens portrayed these women sympathetically. He understood that women like Nancy became prostitutes out of economic necessity; they were poor and had few opportunities to earn a decent living. And he had compassion for women like Agnes, Oliver's mother, who were seduced and abandoned by men who deceived them with promises of marriage. His sympathetic portrayal of these fallen women is an indictment of the hypocrisy and injustice Dickens deplored in his society.

In spite of Nancy's life of crime and vice—not only prostitution, but a drinking problem—something good survives in her. "The girl's life had been squandered in the streets, and among the most noisome stews and dens of London, but there was something of the woman's original nature left in her still…" (Chapter 40). While this stereotype implies that women are naturally more caring and self-sacrificing than men, it does offer a positive view of the values entrusted to women in Victorian society (and in our own as well): connection, nurturance, compassion. And it suggests that perhaps these values are what is lacking in a cold and uncaring society.

With Oliver back in his clutches, Fagin steps up his efforts to corrupt the boy and sends him on a big house-breaking job with Sikes. Oliver gets another chance to escape when the burglary is botched, and he's left behind at the Maylies' home with a gunshot wound. Once again he's under the protection of respectable, upper-class benefactors, and life appears peaceful and almost idyllic.

But danger still looms. There is a very strange nightmarish scene (Chapter 34 in the novel) where Oliver is half-way between dreaming and waking, and he sees Monks and Fagin leering in his window at the cottage. This recalls an earlier scene, Oliver's first morning with the gang (Chapter 9), when he's in a similar half-waking state and observes Fagin gloating over his treasure. When Fagin sees that Oliver is awake and watching him, he terrifies Oliver by threatening him with a knife. The nightmarish, almost surreal, quality of these scenes, along with the clear connection between them, gives them a psychological intensity that seems to suggest a deeper connection between Oliver and the criminal gang, and between the two worlds they represent.

WE'LL GET HOLD OF MONKS. GET HIS SECRET. OTHERWISE, YOU'LL HAVE TO DELIVER UP FAGIN.

NEVER!.. DEVIL THO HE IS! NO ONE MUST BE HARMED, SAVE MONKS! LISTEN AND I'LL TELL YOU WHERE YOU CAN FIND HIM, WHAT HE LOOKS LIKE.

The scenes of Oliver's life with Mr. Brownlow and then with the Maylies are less realistic than those in the criminal underworld. They have the feel of romantic wish-fulfillment: the motherly Mrs. Bedwin, the almost-magical portrait of Agnes, the beautiful Rose, the idyllic cottage—and of course, the outrageous coincidences that have brought Oliver miraculously back into the bosom of his own long-lost family. Dickens didn't expect his readers to see this as realistic. Coincidence is a literary convention that carries symbolic meanings: we are meant to contemplate the ways in which the different classes in society are interconnected. We are also meant to think about virtue and vice and the role they play in human destiny. The use of coincidence is also an indication that Dickens was experimenting with literary forms, combining older traditions with new forms, so that we get a mixture of fairy-tale romance and gritty urban realism, along with comedy, melodrama and satire.

Once Oliver is established in his new home, the focus of the action in the second half of the novel shifts away from Oliver to the adults who are battling over him. The boy who started out as a penniless orphan is now very much in demand. Just who is this boy? Mr. Brownlow sets out to solve the mystery of Oliver's identity, and everyone else seems to have a stake in Oliver as well. Fagin and Monks plot to corrupt Oliver, and Fagin enlists Noah Claypole as his spy. Mr. Brownlow and Rose Maylie join forces to look out for Oliver's interests. Nancy goes to great lengths to protect Oliver from the plot by drugging Sikes so that she can sneak out to warn Rose Maylie of Oliver's danger. Even Mr. Bumble and his wife get into the act by trying to cash in on the information they have about Oliver's mother. Bumble goes first to Mr. Brownlow and then to Monks, selling information to the highest bidder.

At the climax of the book the plot shifts again, to focus on the fates of Nancy, Sikes, and Fagin. The narrative reverts to a more realistic mode, interspersed with some intensely melodramatic moments. The writing becomes more powerful, the tone more urgent, the scenes more compelling.

Fagin makes sure that Sikes finds out about Nancy's efforts to help Oliver, knowing that Sikes will see this as a betrayal, and that he will probably react violently. From what we know about Fagin, it's safe to assume that he wants both Nancy and Sikes dead so that they can never testify against him.

The suspense mounts in the scene where Nancy sneaks out at midnight to meet Rose Maylie and Mr. Brownlow on London Bridge. Unbeknownst to her, she's being followed by Noah Claypole, who is spying for Fagin. We know at this point that she's doomed, and her brutal murder follows soon after.

Sikes is in a daze after killing Nancy, horrified by the blood and gore and by Nancy's dead eyes staring at him. He throws a rug over the body, but "it was worse to fancy the eyes, and imaging them moving toward him…" (Chapter 48). Sikes flees from the scene of his crime and wanders for days in torment, an utter outcast. Eventually he returns to London, and in a bizarre and gruesome scene he is hounded to his death by an angry mob.

The next-to-last chapter, "Fagin's Last Night Alive," is another intensely dramatized scene. In it, we get a kind of stream-of-consciousness account of Fagin's state of mind as he faces execution.

Meanwhile, the details of Oliver's happy ending are being worked out: he's adopted by Mr. Brownlow and he will inherit money from his father. Harry Maylie gives up his political ambitions so that Rose will consent to marry him. The happy ending is a romantic convention, expected by Dickens's audience—but it seems almost like an afterthought to us when compared to the chilling realism of the violent fates of the criminals. These are the scenes that we remember long after we have finished the book. Dickens's ability to enter into the minds of his criminal characters and his vivid representation of their misery and desperation are an important part of what makes *Oliver Twist* a great book.

Study Questions

•Many characters' names in *Oliver Twist* seem to have significance; consider the name that Mr. Bumble gives Oliver: "Twist," a prediction that he'll hang on the gallows. What other characters' names are significant in light of their personalities or fates?

•Compare Nancy and Rose. How are they different? How are they the same? What stereotypes of women do they represent? Which woman do you find a more satisfying "heroine" for the book?

•Consider one (or more) of the social problems dramatized in *Oliver Twist* in light of how it affects a given character. How much control does the character over his/her own life and problems?

•Which characters in the novel appear to be entirely products of their environment? Which characters act in ways that environment alone does not explain?

•Food is an important theme in this book. Which characters are associated with starvation? Which ones with feasting? Who has no appetite? Who eats with pleasure? What does this say about each character?

•In what way does Charlotte's relationship with Noah echo Nancy's relationship with Bill Sikes? In what way does it differ? How do you think Charlotte will end up?

About the Essayist:

A doctoral candidate at the University of California at Santa Cruz, Deborah Condon is a member of The Dickens Project. a consortium of colleges and universities headquartered at UC Santa Cruz.